DISCOVER!

CALLING ALL COMMUNITY HEROES!

WHO ANSWERS 911 CALLS?

BY THERESA EMMINIZER

Enslow PUBLISHING

Please visit our website, www.enslow.com.
For a free color catalog of all our high-quality books, call toll free 1-800-398-2504 or fax 1-877-980-4454.

Library of Congress Cataloging-in-Publication Data
Names: Emminizer, Theresa, author.
Title: Who answers 911 calls? / Theresa Emminizer.
Description: Buffalo, New York : Enslow Publishing, [2025] | Series: Calling all community heroes! | Includes index.
Identifiers: LCCN 2024022637 (print) | LCCN 2024022638 (ebook) | ISBN 9781978542136 (library binding) | ISBN 9781978542129 (paperback) | ISBN 9781978542143 (ebook)
Subjects: LCSH: Emergency communication systems–Juvenile literature. | Telephone–Emergency reporting systems–Juvenile literature.
Classification: LCC HV551.25 .E56 2025 (print) | LCC HV551.25 (ebook) | DDC 384.6/4–dc23/eng/20240715
LC record available at https://lccn.loc.gov/2024022637
LC ebook record available at https://lccn.loc.gov/2024022638

Published in 2025 by
Enslow Publishing
2544 Clinton Street
Buffalo, NY 14224

Designer: Tanya Dellaccio Keeney
Editor: Theresa Emminizer

Photo credits: Cover (background) ASTA DESIGN/Shutterstock.com; cover (speech bubble) mejorana/Shutterstock.com; cover (person) MNBB Studio/Shutterstock.com; cover (phone) Simon Vayro/Shutterstock.com; p. 5 CrispyPork/Shutterstock.com; p. 7 Elena Berd/Shutterstock.com; p. 9 Mircea Moira/Shutterstock.com; p. 11 antoniodiaz/Shutterstock.com; p. 13 Olha Nosova/Shutterstock.com; p. 15 fizkes/Shutterstock.com; p. 17 AS photo family/Shutterstock.com; p. 19 Hryshchyshen Serhii/Shutterstock.com; p. 21 PeopleImages.com - Yuri A/Shutterstock.com.

Printed in the United States of America

Some of the images in this book illustrate individuals who are models. The depictions do not imply actual situations or events.

CPSIA compliance information: Batch #CWENS25: For further information contact Enslow Publishing, at 1-800-398-2504.

CONTENTS

BOLDFACE WORDS APPEAR IN WORDS TO KNOW.

QUICK, CALL 911!

In an **emergency**, call 911! That's the number for emergencies in the United States. People who answer 911 calls are called operators or dispatchers. They ask questions. They send help. Emergencies are scary, but 911 operators help keep people safe!

MOST CELL PHONES HAVE AN "EMERGENCY CALL" BUTTON. YOU CAN PRESS THIS TO CALL 911 EVEN IF THE PHONE IS LOCKED.

WHO'S ON THE LINE?

The people who answer 911 calls are sometimes police officers or firefighters. Sometimes they are simply people from the community who do very important work! To become a 911 operator, a person must have a high school degree, or have finished high school.

THIS SIGN THANKS ESSENTIAL, OR NECESSARY, WORKERS, SUCH AS 911 OPERATORS.

AN OPERATOR'S JOB

To become 911 operators, people must go through special training. They need to pass tests as well as **background checks**. Operators need to be able to stay calm and gather **information** very quickly. They enter the information into a computer and send the proper emergency **response team** to the scene.

OPERATORS WHO ANSWER 911 CALLS WORK IN 911 CALL CENTERS.

WHEN TO CALL

When should you call 911?

You should call when:

- there is a fire
- someone is badly hurt
- someone turns blue, can't breathe, or can't talk
- someone is passed out
- someone is in danger
- a crime is happening
- you're in a car crash

NEVER CALL 911 AS A JOKE. IF YOU CALL BY MISTAKE, DON'T HANG UP! TELL THE OPERATOR WHAT HAPPENED.

WHAT WILL HAPPEN?

A 911 operator will answer your call. They'll ask you questions. Try to answer as calmly as you can. Remember, operators want to help you! They'll ask questions like:

- "What is your emergency?"
- "Where are you? "
- "Who is with you?"

IF YOU DON'T KNOW WHERE YOU ARE, LOOK FOR **LANDMARKS** THAT WILL HELP EMERGENCY WORKERS FIND YOU.

STAY ON THE LINE

Don't hang up! The operator will tell you what to do while you wait for help to arrive. They may tell you to move to a safer place. They may tell you how to help someone who is sick or hurt.

TELL THE OPERATOR EVERYTHING YOU CAN ABOUT WHAT'S GOING ON.

HELP IS ON THE WAY!

The operator will send different emergency response teams to you based on what is going on. If there is a crime, the police will come. If there is a fire, firefighters will come. If someone is sick or hurt, an **ambulance** and emergency **medical team** will help.

THE 911 OPERATOR TELLS THE EMERGENCY RESPONSE TEAM WHAT IS GOING ON.

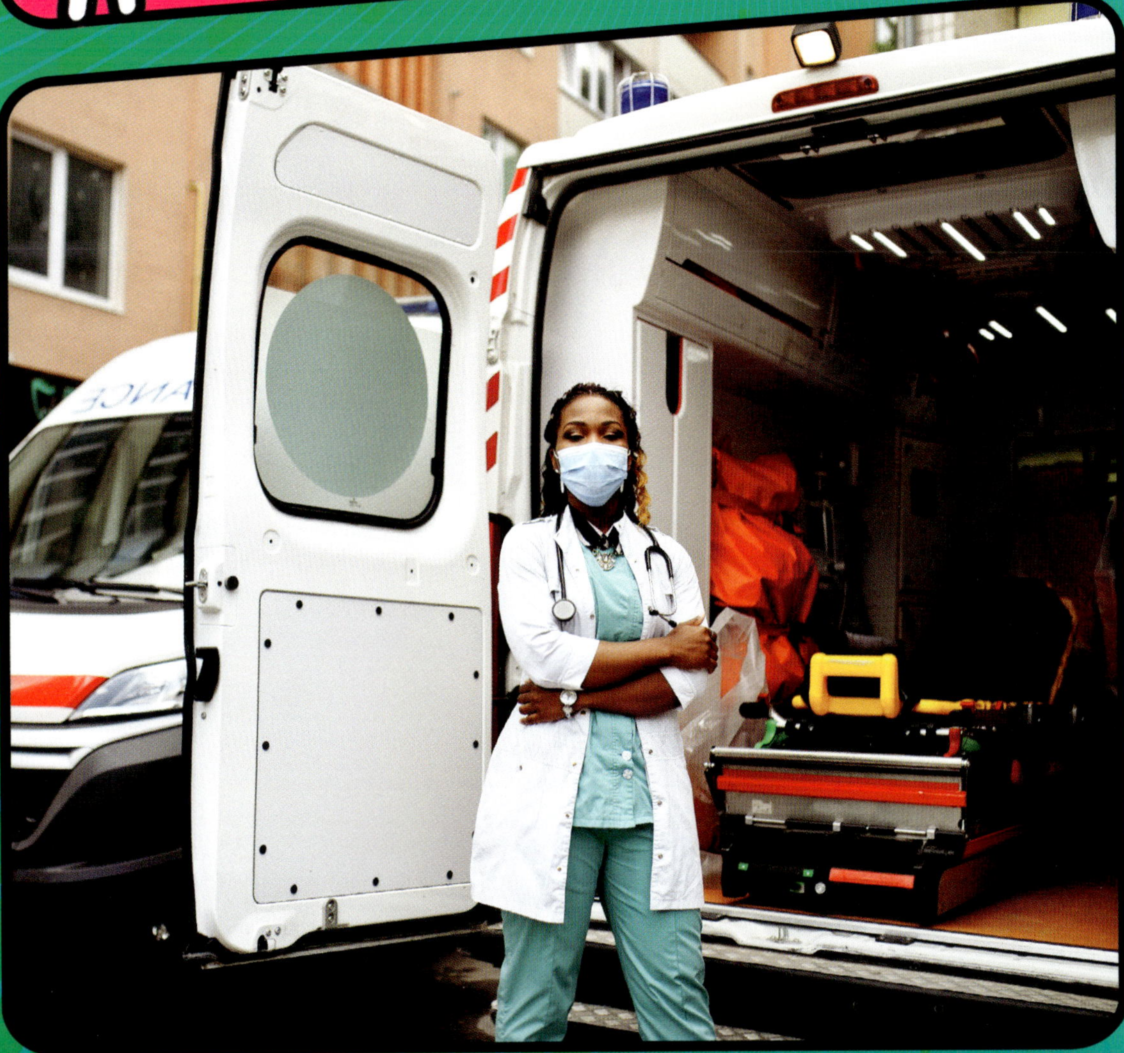

WHAT HAPPENS NEXT?

The 911 operator will not hang up the phone until you get the help you need. They may stay on the line until a team reaches you. Or they may **transfer** your call to an emergency responder who can help you better.

EMERGENCY RESPONDERS WILL TAKE CARE OF YOU.

COMMUNITY HEROES

People who answer 911 calls are heroes! They are the first people you talk to in an emergency. They are calm, think quickly, and are able to help you through all sorts of different scary events. Operators who answer 911 calls make your community a safer place!

THE PEOPLE WHO ANSWER 911 CALLS SAVE LIVES EVERY DAY.

WORDS TO KNOW

ambulance: A vehicle that takes people to the hospital when they are sick or hurt.

background check: A process involving looking into someone's life or actions before they start a new job.

emergency: An unexpected situation that needs quick action.

information: Facts or knowledge about something.

landmark: Something around you that is easy to see and recognize, such as a building, tree, or body of water.

medical team: A team of workers who give health or medical care. Medical care is care given by doctors.

response team: A team of workers who deal with emergencies.

transfer: To cause something, such as a call, to move from one person or place to another

FOR MORE INFORMATION

BOOKS

Jensen Shaffer, Jody. *911 Dispatchers on the Call*. Mankato, MN: The Child's World, 2022.

Sipperley, Keli. *Ambulances*. North Mankato, MN: Pebble, a Capstone imprint, 2022.

WEBSITES

Nemours KidsHealth
kidshealth.org/en/kids/911.html
Read this helpful page about when to call 911.

911 for Kids
911forkids.com/
Find facts about 911 and read safety tips on 911 for Kids.

Publisher's note to educators and parents: Our editors have carefully reviewed these websites to ensure that they are suitable for students. Many websites change frequently, however, and we cannot guarantee that a site's future contents will continue to meet our high standards of quality and educational value. Be advised that students should be closely supervised whenever they access the internet.

INDEX